A Note From Denise Renner

The Word of God is so powerful in our lives. It is essential that every person spend time with God and study His Word in order to stay spiritually strong in these last days.

This study guide corresponds to my *TIME With Denise Renner* TV program by the same title that can be viewed at **deniserenner.org**. My desire is that through these lessons, you find the encouragement and freedom in Christ that you need. I believe the Holy Spirit is going to speak to you through the words you read in this study tool and that as you begin to use it, you will be *propelled* into the abundant life God has planned for you. I encourage you to make the effort to receive all He has for you and all He wants to do in you — it will definitely be worth it!

Whether you have walked with the Lord a long time or have just begun to follow Him, there is so much He wants to give you from His Word. He sees where you are, and He wants to meet you there.

> Therefore do not worry about tomorrow, for tomorrow
> will worry about its own things.
> Sufficient for the day is its own trouble.
> — Matthew 6:34

Your sister and friend in Jesus Christ,

Denise Renner

Unless otherwise indicated, all scripture quotations are taken from the *New King James Version®*. Copyright © 1982 by Thomas Nelson. Used by permission. All rights reserved.

Scripture quotations marked (*AMPC*) are taken from the *Amplified® Bible, Classic Edition*. Copyright © 1954, 1958, 1962, 1964, 1965, 1987 by The Lockman Foundation. Used by permission. www.Lockman.org.

Scripture quotations marked (*KJV*) are taken from the *King James Version* of the Bible.

Scripture quotations marked (*NIV*) are taken from *Holy Bible, New International Version®, NIV®* Copyright ©1973, 1978, 1984, 2011 by Biblica, Inc.® Used by permission. All rights reserved worldwide.

Scripture quotations marked (*NLT*) are taken from the Holy Bible, *New Living Translation*, copyright © 1996, 2004, 2015 by Tyndale House Foundation. Used by permission of Tyndale House Publishers, Inc., Carol Stream, Illinois 60188. All rights reserved.

Scripture quotations marked (*TLB*) are taken from *The Living Bible* copyright © 1971. Used by permission of Tyndale House Publishers, Inc., Carol Stream, Illinois 60188. All rights reserved.

It's Not Over Till It's Over

Copyright © 2024 by Denise Renner
1814 W. Tacoma St.
Broken Arrow, OK 74012-1406

Published by Rick Renner Ministries
www.renner.org

ISBN 13: 978-1-6675-0744-6

ISBN 13 eBook: 978-1-6675-0745-3

All rights reserved. No portion of this book may be reproduced or transmitted in any form or by any means — electronic, mechanical, photocopy, recording, scanning, or other (except for brief quotations in critical reviews or articles) — without the prior written permission of the Publisher.

LESSON 1

TOPIC
No Fear in Death

SCRIPTURES
1. **1 Corinthians 15:55-57** — "O Death, where is your sting? O Hades, where is your victory?" The sting of death is sin, and the strength of sin is the law. But thanks be to God, who gives us the victory through our Lord Jesus Christ.

SYNOPSIS
The five lessons in this study on *It's Not Over Till It's Over* will focus on the following topics:

- No Fear in Death
- Words of Life Have Power Over Death
- Death Knocks, But Jesus Answers
- Forgiveness Opens the Door to the Impossible
- Don't Just Hold On to the Power — Give It Away!

The times in which we live can be quite tiresome and taxing, and the desire to give up can become overwhelming. Yet despite the mounting difficulties, God offers us His grace to press forward and be unstoppable! With His empowerment, we can push past anxiety and fear, reject the opportunities to be offended, and turn a deaf ear to the negative opinions of others. The fact is, *it's not over till God says it's over!*

The emphasis of this lesson:

Heather Z joins Denise Renner and shares her death-to-life story — how at age 12 she died, went to Heaven, and came face to face with the person of Jesus! Her life demonstrates that for believers, there is no fear in death because Christ has removed its sting.

Heather Z's Story

Never underestimate the power of God inside your life. Scripture says, "...[He] is able to do exceedingly abundantly above all that we ask or think, according to the power that works in us" (Ephesians 3:20). Here is what Heather Z shared about how God's power worked in her to supernaturally bring her back to life after experiencing a fatal injury.

> From seven years old until my senior year in high school, I was seriously involved in gymnastics. I remember a time when I was 12 and some ministry friends of my parents were visiting. I was asked to take their daughter to the park. I had just finished about four hours of gymnastics practice, and my muscles were really stressed and tired. But that didn't matter. In my little mind, everything was fine, so I took this younger girl with me to the park, and we began to play.
>
> I saw the parallel bars, and I ran over to them and lifted myself up with my shoulders. I wasn't doing anything wild or outrageous — I was just swinging back and forth and was only about two inches off the ground. Unfortunately, I didn't realize how stressed my muscles were from the four hours of gymnastics, and at some point while I was swinging back, my muscles spasmed in such a way that I flew forward off the parallel bars and hit my head on the concrete slab on the ground. Instantly, my neck snapped back, and I heard a loud crack, and then everything went black.
>
> Moments later, I began to awaken and realized I was lying on the ground. The little girl I had brought with me was looking down at me and was crying.
>
> "What should I do?" she sobbed.
>
> With much effort, I mustered the words, "Go get my parents."
>
> At that point, I must have blacked out again, and the next thing I remember was I was walking down the street toward the house, having no idea how I got there. When I finally reached the house, I walked into the room where my parents were, and I was holding my neck.
>
> "Are you alright?" my mom asked.

"I think I broke my neck," I said. I was in so much shock I could barely shed a single tear. Strangely, I wasn't in any pain — just a bit of throbbing. The jolt had left me so traumatized that my whole body became numb.

Rushed to the Hospital

Immediately, my parents got me in the car and drove me straight to the hospital, and upon arrival, my father went in and told the staff, "I think my daughter broke her neck."

"Where is she?" they exclaimed.

"She's in the car," he responded.

"You moved her?" they retorted in disbelief.

"Actually, she walked home," he informed them.

Quickly, the workers came and got me and brought me inside, asking me all kinds of questions to try to determine the severity of my injuries. After testing my vision and cognitive abilities, they wheeled me down to the X-ray room and positioned me for a series of pictures to be taken.

What I didn't know at the time was that I had broken the very top vertebra in my neck, which is called C1. It's the same vertebrae that the actor Christopher Reeves broke in a horse-riding accident that left him paralyzed from the neck down.

When a person breaks C1, it greatly affects their lungs and the ability to breathe. It's considered "hangman's vertebra" because when a person hangs himself, C1 is what breaks, cutting off their airflow and causing them to suffocate to death.

From Death to Life

So there I was, lying on the table waiting for the technicians to take the X-rays. After the nurse got me situated, she told me she would be right back and then left the room. The next thing I knew I was floating above my body, looking down at myself laying on the table. In that moment, I had died — but I had no fear whatsoever.

As I seemed to hover in mid-air, I remember thinking, *That's me on that table.*

Then suddenly I left the hospital room and went to a beautiful place that I knew was my home, but it was in Heaven, not on earth. While I was there, I saw several people that I knew had already passed, but I couldn't speak to them. I could only watch as they fellowshipped with each other, which was wonderful to see.

I then turned my head and looked out the window of my home where I saw indescribably lush vegetation. The colors were incredibly vibrant, and the giant green blades of grass were more extraordinary than anything I'd ever seen in my life.

Looking even further into the distance, I saw beautiful heads of wheat, but unlike the wheat I had seen on earth, this wheat was gold and seemed to radiate golden light. As I was looking out at these vast fields of vegetation, I lifted my eyes up into the sky, and I saw what looked like two huge hands that began to fill the heavens. Suddenly, those huge hands swooped down and cupped together under me, bearing me up in great strength.

Hearing God's Voice

I then heard a voice begin to speak to me, and it was the voice of the Lord.

What's interesting is that when He spoke, I heard Him internally. Likewise, when I spoke to Him, I didn't use my mouth to talk; I simply *thought* my response. We communicated with each other spirit to spirit, which confirms what the Bible says. When we are born again, our spirit is connected to God's Spirit, and we become one spirit (*see* 1 Corinthians 6:17).

As the Lord spoke to me, I remember Him telling me things about my life. But what I will never forget is when He said, "Heather, there's going to be a time in the future when I'm going to come to you and remind you of this experience, and you're going to need it. But don't worry; everything is going to be okay. I have you in the palm of My hands."

In that moment, I remember trying to look at His face, but it was so brilliant, I couldn't see anything. Then once more, the Lord said to me, "Heather, don't worry. Everything's going to be okay. I have you in My hands. But now it's time for you to go."

"No, please," I said. "I don't want to go. I don't want to go."

But the Lord just said again, "Heather, don't worry. Everything's going to be okay. I have you in My hands. I have many assignments for you. It's time for you to go."

A Little Girl With No Halo

The next thing I remember was opening my eyes and being on the table back in the hospital. As wind rushed into my lungs, I suddenly inhaled deeply and started breathing again.

Now it just so happens that in that city on that particular day, there was a renowned doctor who specialized in dealing with the kind of injury I had. He had been in town conducting a big conference and was on his way to the airport when he realized he had forgotten his pager, and he returned to the hospital to retrieve it. That in itself was a miracle because doctors in that day didn't normally misplace their pagers.

Fortunately for me, coming back to the hospital caused him to miss his flight and placed him in the emergency area while I was there. The staff learned of his return and immediately reached out to him for his expert advice.

"You're not going to believe this," they said, "but we have a little girl in here who broke her neck. Would you look at her X-rays because we're thinking about doing a halo procedure on her?"

A halo procedure is where they drill holes into a person's skull and attach a metal cage around the person's head that rests on the shoulders in hopes of immobilizing the neck so that it can fully heal. That is what the doctors were about ready to do to me.

So, the specialist said, "Okay, let me see the X-rays."

With a perplexed look on his face, he said, "I've never seen anything like this before. These X-rays clearly show she broke her neck, but they also show that C1 has somehow been fused back together."

Keep in mind that no invasive medical procedures had been done on me — only X-rays. The specialist then said, "This girl doesn't need holes drilled in her head and a halo. She just needs a soft collar for six weeks, and she'll be fine."

What had happened was an absolute miracle. God brought my dead body back to life and fused my broken bones!

For the Believer, There Is No Fear in Death!

The world we live in is a diluted, pale comparison to the real world that awaits us. The eternal, spiritual dimension is far more vibrant and more real than anything we've ever seen in this life. If we will turn our eyes upon Jesus, as the old song says, and look full into His wonderful face, the things of this earth will grow strangely dim in the light of His glory and grace.

Friend, there is no fear in death. Like Heather, believers who have tasted death and seen the other side, can testify that in the life that is to come, there's no pain, no anxiety, no worry, and no fear. Everything is more real, and life is full of indescribable joy and wonder. Relationships, conversations, and how people interact with each other are far better than anything we could imagine.

The veil — or separation — between the physical realm in which we live and the eternal, spiritual realm of Heaven is very thin, and there's nothing to be afraid of when you know Jesus and He's the Lord of your life.

Through Christ's death on the Cross and His triumphant resurrection from the grave, He defeated death once and for all! The apostle Paul celebrated the victory we have through Jesus' finished work in First Corinthians 15:55-57, where he wrote:

> **So when this corruptible has put on incorruption, and this mortal has put on immortality, then shall be brought to pass the saying that is written: "Death is swallowed up in victory."**
>
> **"O Death, where is your sting? O Hades, where is your victory?"**
>
> **The sting of death is sin, and the strength of sin is the law. But thanks be to God, who gives us the victory through our Lord Jesus Christ.**

Jesus conquered death, and it no longer has any power over us! When Heather died at age 12, she effortlessly transitioned from life to death to life, and death had no fear and no sting. She went from earth to Heaven in an instant by the power of God. Most people live their life tormented by the fear of dying, but if you're a believer, there is no fear in death.

What God Says Is What He Does

The Bible says to be absent from the body is to be present with the Lord (*see* 2 Corinthians 5:8). When Heather crossed over from death to life with Jesus, she was strengthened by His presence and encouraged by His words. The Lord's instructions produced an indescribable peace that flooded her heart, her mind, and her entire being. And that superior sense of safety and security went with Heather when her spirit returned to her physical body back in the hospital.

Although she really didn't want to leave God's presence, when He said it was time to go, she went, knowing He had many more assignments for her. That word of God that came to Heather at age 12 is still being fulfilled in her life to this day.

Friend, if God has spoken something to you in the past and it seems like an impossibility, don't cast it away. Hold tightly to what He said — He's not a man that he should lie or change His mind about what He said (*see* Numbers 23:19). What He said He will do.

We Are No Longer Slaves to the Fear of Death!

If you've been afraid of dying and you're a Christian, you need a deeper revelation of God's immense love for you and what Christ did for you on the Cross. There's no fear in death, for the very sting of death has been destroyed by Jesus. The writer of Hebrews tells us:

> **Because God's children are human beings — made of flesh and blood — the Son also became flesh and blood. For only as a human being could he die, and only by dying could he break the power of the devil, who had the power of death. Only in this way could he set free all who have lived their lives as slaves to the fear of dying.**
> — **Hebrews 2:14,15** *NLT*

Friend, the power of death and the fear of dying have been destroyed, and it's not because of our goodness, our confessing the Word, or anything else we can do. The sting of death was conquered because of Jesus' finished work — His death, burial, and resurrection.

God wants us to receive all that is ours through Jesus and live this life to the very fullest, which means knowing Jesus as intimately as we can, loving God with all our heart, and loving people and bringing them to Him. The life we live in our physical body is our opportunity to serve Jesus, giving Him all that we are.

"So be careful how you live. Don't live like fools, but like those who are wise. Make the most of every opportunity in these evil days" (Ephesians 5:15,16 *NLT*). Show Jesus. Share Jesus. Live fearlessly!

STUDY QUESTIONS
Be diligent to present yourself approved to God, a worker who does not need to be ashamed, rightly dividing the word of truth.
— 2 Timothy 2:15

1. What God says in His Word is powerful and can be trusted. To help strengthen your trust in God's Word, take some time to meditate on these verses and commit them to memory:
   - Numbers 23:19
   - 1 Kings 8:56
   - Matthew 5:18
   - Luke 21:33 (Also Matthew 24:35)
   - Hebrews 6:18

2. The Bible says that Jesus defeated the devil and destroyed the fear of death for those who believe in Him. To better understand what Christ accomplished, carefully read Hebrews 2:14-18 and Hebrews 4:15 and 16. What is the Holy Spirit showing you in these passages?

PRACTICAL APPLICATION
But be doers of the word, and not hearers only, deceiving yourselves.
— James 1:22

1. What stands out most to you from Heather Z's personal life-to-death-to-life story?
2. Have you — or someone close to you — ever had such an experience? If so, what was it like? How has it impacted your life?
3. If you're struggling with fear, begin to pray and ask the Holy Spirit to give you a deeper, personal revelation of God's love for you. Remember, "There is no fear in love [dread does not exist], but full-grown (complete, perfect) love turns fear out of doors and expels every trace of terror…" (1 John 4:18 *AMPC*).

LESSON 2

TOPIC
Words of Life Have Power Over Death

SCRIPTURES
1. **Matthew 10:7,8** — And as you go, preach, saying, 'The kingdom of heaven is at hand.' Heal the sick, cleanse the lepers, raise the dead, cast out demons. Freely you have received, freely give.
2. **Luke 7:12-15** — And when He came near the gate of the city, behold, a dead man was being carried out, the only son of his mother; and she was a widow. And a large crowd from the city was with her. When the Lord saw her, He had compassion on her and said to her, "Do not weep." Then He came and touched the open coffin, and those who carried him stood still. And He said, "Young man, I say to you, arise." So he who was dead sat up and began to speak. And He presented him to his mother.
3. **1 Corinthians 15:55-57** — "O Death, where is your sting? O Hades, where is your victory?" The sting of death is sin, and the strength of sin is the law. But thanks be to God, who gives us the victory through our Lord Jesus Christ.

SYNOPSIS

If you are a born-again follower of Jesus, the Bible says your body has become the temple of the Holy Spirit (*see* 1 Corinthians 3:16). And according to Romans 8:11, the same mighty Spirit that raised Christ from the dead is living in you! That means you have the death-defeating resurrection power of Jesus living inside you, and you take Him with you everywhere you go!

One of the greatest ways we release God's power is through our words. Proverbs 18:21 says, "Death and life are in the power of the tongue...." So what kind of words are you speaking? Are they words of fear, doubt, and negativity? Or are they life-giving words founded on God's Word? It's our words of life that detonate power over all forms of death, as we'll see in this lesson.

The emphasis of this lesson:

After three days of no movement from the baby in Heather's womb, her husband, Joseph Z, spoke words of life over the baby, and God raised the child back to life! In the same way, God wants us to be a pipeline through which His power flows, using our words to release life.

A Brief Review of Lesson 1

In our first lesson, Heather Z shared her testimony of how she had broken her neck at the age of 12 and died. While absent from her physical body, God took her to Heaven, spoke to her about her life, and informed her that He had specific assignments for her to carry out. He then returned her spirit and soul to her body and miraculously healed her neck by fusing the broken bones back together.

The specialist who happened to return to the hospital while Heather was there noted that her X-rays showed her C1 vertebrae had indeed been broken, but somehow it had been fused back together. Through it all, Heather was not afraid. The sting of death had been swallowed by the finished work of Jesus Christ!

We, too, are not to be afraid of death because Jesus has conquered it (*see* Hebrews 2:14,15). Regardless of the troubles and trials we face in this life, the Bible says, "Yet in all these things we are more than conquerors through Him who loved us" (Romans 8:37).

Just as Jesus Is All About Life, We Are To Be All About Life Too

In today's world, we are surrounded by elements of death. Just turn on the TV, power up your computer, or scan the headlines on your phone or tablet. It's all about death. News of increased natural disasters, widespread robberies, more murders, and new threats of nuclear war are popping up everywhere. These are all elements of death.

But Jesus is all about life! He conquered death, and He is the Greater One living inside you (*see* 1 John 4:4). The ministry of life He began 2,000 years ago is to continue through us — His Church — until the end of the age. When Jesus sent out His 12 disciples, He told them, "…Preach, saying, 'The kingdom of heaven is at hand.' Heal the sick, cleanse the lepers, raise the dead, cast out demons. Freely you have received, freely give" (Matthew 10:7,8).

Although the times are constantly changing, Christ's mission remains the same. Empowered by His mighty Spirit, we are essentially to preach — or announce — the Good News of Jesus to others and then demonstrate His Kingdom by healing the sick, cleansing the diseased, casting out devils, and yes, even raising the dead.

Jesus is the SAME yesterday, today, and forever (*see* Hebrews 13:8). What He and His disciples did then, He desires to do now. Our part is to be ready and to make ourselves available for His Spirit to flow through us. We're the "pipe" through which His power flows, and nothing is impossible for Him!

Raising the Dead in Jesus' Name Is in the Job Description of a Believer

Again and again in Scripture, it seems that Jesus was drawn to those who were desperate and dealing with issues of death. The gospel of Luke records such an event when the Lord was traveling through a town and came upon a funeral for a young man. The Bible says:

> **Now it happened, the day after, that He went into a city called Nain; and many of His disciples went with Him, and a large crowd.**

And when He came near the gate of the city, behold, a dead man was being carried out, the only son of his mother; and she was a widow. And a large crowd from the city was with her.

When the Lord saw her, He had compassion on her and said to her, "Do not weep." Then He came and touched the open coffin, and those who carried him stood still. And He said, "Young man, I say to you, arise." So he who was dead sat up and began to speak. And He presented him to his mother.

— Luke 7:11-15

In Jesus' day, widows, like the one in this story who had no children, often ended up becoming beggars with no one to take care of them. Jesus was aware of the woman's plight and was moved with compassion to take action. Thus, He stepped into this woman's desperate, death-filled situation, stepped up to the casket, and released *life* through the words of His mouth.

Death obeyed the voice of Jesus and let go of the woman's son. He came back to life, which restored the woman's hope and future and moved the people to give God great glory (*see* Luke 7:16). That's the resurrection power of Jesus! It is the same identical power living inside us.

Friend, we are living in desperate times in which serious situations abound. It could be that the Spirit of God may call upon you to open your mouth, speak words of life, and raise someone from the dead. You may have thought that such miraculous manifestations were confined to the canon of Scripture, but they are not. Jesus was — and always will be — the Resurrection and the Life (*see* John 11:25). And if you are willing, He will move through you to bring resurrection and life to those in need around you.

A Modern-Day Resurrection

Heather Z and her husband, Joseph, have had many unique experiences with the Lord, and one of those experiences occurred in connection with the pregnancy of their daughter, Allison. Here is the story Heather shared:

> I was expecting and was about six months along in the pregnancy, and that baby was moving all around and kicking everywhere inside me. But all that movement came to a standstill, and I felt nothing for three days. Then late one night I began experiencing severe

stomach pain. Concerned, I called my doctor, and she told me to go to the emergency room right away, which is what I did.

As soon as we arrived, they quickly sent me into the emergency room, and they started running all sorts of tests. They then put the little device over my stomach and began to conduct an ultrasound to see how the baby was doing.

At that time, we were in our early twenties — just young babies having babies. As my husband, Joseph, was sitting beside me, he jokingly commented to the technician, "Wow! I bet you see a lot of things when you're doing these ultrasounds."

"Oh yes," he said. "I see many things in here, but because I'm only a technician and not a doctor, I don't have the authority to tell patients what's going on. Sometimes I see dead babies, but I can't say anything because it's not my place."

Little did we know that he was trying to tell us something without officially telling us. But we were so young and naïve, we just said, "Oh, that must be terrible for you," not thinking that he could be referring to us.

Well, after they ran all the tests, I could tell the doctors were very somber and sad. They then began the discharge process and said, "We're going to look at your test results and then talk to your doctor, and she'll call you in the morning and let you know what you need to do."

"Okay," we responded nonchalantly, and we went home.

After I had been sitting on the couch for a while, Joseph came over to me and said, "I need to pray, and I need to speak over this baby."

"Absolutely," I said. "Let's do that."

So he laid his hands on my stomach and began to say, "Jesus, I speak life into this baby. I command life to flow into this child and say that this baby will live and be healthy and strong and full of God and full of faith and peace."

At that time, neither of us knew the seriousness of the situation we were dealing with. All we knew was that I was having severe stomach pain, and my husband just wanted to make sure I wasn't going to go into labor too early.

So as he prayed, I prayed and agreed with him for God to do what we asked, and that was it. Just a short prayer for our baby, and then we went to bed. The next morning as I got up and was getting ready for the day, suddenly, I saw an elbow run across my stomach and then a little foot. Then I started feeling kicking and all kinds of activity in my belly.

Shortly thereafter, I got a call from my doctor.

"I'm so sorry for your loss," she said somberly. "These things happen, and it's not your fault. If you need counseling to work through the death of your child, we're here for you and we will help you go through the process."

Apparently, my doctor had looked at the findings from the ultrasound and all the various tests from the previous day, all of which showed that our baby had died.

In utter disbelief, I said, "That's impossible! This baby is kicking all over inside my stomach."

"What?" the doctor exclaimed. "Oh, my goodness! We need to do some more tests!"

Sure enough, our baby was alive. And she's now 22 years old! Her name is Allison, and she's a beautiful girl, full of life and filled with the Spirit of God!

Friend, that is the resurrection power of Jesus Christ at work! When Joseph and Heather prayed, the Spirit of God living on the inside of them released power into their baby, and she was raised back to life! Their prayers were answered — not because *they* are so good, but because *God* is so good. Jesus conquered death, hell, and the grave through His finished work, and in his Name, we too have authority over death.

Speak Life to What's Dead in Your Life!

It may be that you are dealing with one or more things that seem to be dead in your life. It may be that an aspect of your health has died, or your finances are on life support. Or it may be that you are experiencing a dead marriage or the relationship you have with one or more of your children is numb and lifeless.

Whatever the case may be, *it's not over until God says it's over!* The Greater One lives inside of you, and you can SPEAK LIFE to any of these kinds of situations and experience a supernatural resurrection! Sure, things may look very bleak and impossible to turn around, "…But with God all things are possible" (Matthew 19:26).

So right now, we join our faith with yours and declare words of life over you and your situations.

- We speak LIFE to your marriage.
- We speak LIFE to your relationships with your children and family members.
- We speak LIFE to your limbs and every part of your physical body.
- We speak LIFE to your mind, your emotions, and your will.
- We speak LIFE to your God-given dreams and the future He has prepared for you.

Friend, the power of God is greater than the death that the devil is trying to bring on your body, your soul, your finances, your marriage, and your relationships with family members and friends. And by faith, we release that power *right now* in Jesus' name! May healing and hope, joy and peace, love and laughter come alive in your home, your heart, and in the hearts of your loved ones.

It's through the power of Christ that we can speak with confidence against every form of death. Likewise, in His name, we bind every form of fear coming against you and your family. If you have lost a child, we speak the comforting presence of God to be released in your life and restore your heart. May you experience His wholeness and peace so that there's nothing broken and nothing lacking. May the Spirit of Jesus come alive in your life and release His resurrection power wherever it is needed. In Jesus' name!

STUDY QUESTIONS

Be diligent to present yourself approved to God, a worker who does not need to be ashamed, rightly dividing the word of truth.
— 2 Timothy 2:15

1. According to Mark 16:17 and 18, what five things did Jesus Himself say we would do in His name if we believe? Can you see yourself operating in this resurrection power in these last of the last days?
2. God says, "Death and life are in the power of the tongue…" (Proverbs 18:21). And that includes *your* tongue. The best words of life you can speak are the Scriptures themselves. According to these passages, what are some of the things you can expect to happen when you fill your mind and mouth with God's Word?
   - Hebrews 4:12
   - Jeremiah 5:14; 23:28,29
   - John 15:3 and 17:17

PRACTICAL APPLICATION

But be doers of the word, and not hearers only, deceiving yourselves.
— James 1:22

1. Now more than ever, we need a greater, more expansive understanding of God's power working in and through us. Take some time to meditate on the message of Romans 8:11 and Ephesians 3:20. And ask the Holy Spirit to flood your soul and spirit with a fresh revelation of His matchless anointing inside you.
2. What Jesus and His disciples did in the *past* is what He desires to do through us in the *present*. Get still in God's presence and pray, saying "Lord, am I ready for You to pour Yourself through me to transform others? If not, what can I do to prepare and make myself more available for You to flow through?" Be still and listen. What is the Holy Spirit showing you?

LESSON 3

TOPIC
Death Knocks, But Jesus Answers

SYNOPSIS
As a believer and follower of Jesus, you house the very Spirit of God. Over and over, the apostle Paul says, "…Your body is the temple of the Holy Spirit who is in you, whom you have from God…" (1 Corinthians 6:19). Indeed, "…The Spirit of God, who raised up Jesus from the dead, lives in you…" (Romans 8:11 *TLB*). If you're a Christian, you are power-packed!

Friend, the Spirit of Life living inside you is far greater than any form of death. So regardless of what you are facing or how difficult the situation may be, *hold on in faith*. Whatever form of death is knocking at your door, let Jesus answer it! If you will fall in love with Him and fill your heart and mind with His Word, His Spirit will strengthen you to stay in a place of faith until the problem passes and the miracle manifests.

The emphasis of this lesson:

Heather Z shares how God's love and the truth of His Word carried her through a two-and-a-half-year fight for her life against double kidney failure. From the moment she received the diagnosis to the ongoing dialysis treatments, God was holding her and healing her. She came to know Jesus and learned to believe His Word above her feelings and circumstances.

Death Is No Match for the Lord!

Thus far, Heather Z has shared two stories from her life of how it really looked like it was over, but the Lord stepped in and supernaturally turned death into life. In Lesson 1, we saw that at age 12 she broke her neck, died, and went to Heaven. But then God healed her and sent her back to earth with specific assignments to fulfill.

In Lesson 2, Heather shared how when she was six months pregnant with her first-born child, the baby died in her womb. But through words of life spoken in prayer, her baby came back to life, and now she is 22 years old, full of life, and filled with the Spirit of God!

Friend, death is no match for the Lord! Through Jesus' death, burial, and resurrection, death has been defeated and it no longer has any hold on us. In fact, even the fear of death has been stripped of its power by the finished work of the Cross (*see* Hebrews 2:14,15). Jesus said, "…In the world you will have tribulation; but be of good cheer, I have overcome the world" (John 16:33). Praise God! He is faithful to His Word!

How Are You To Respond When Blindsided With Bad News?

You may have read the account of when Jesus raised Lazarus from the grave. It is His last recorded public display of power before enduring the Cross. What is extremely interesting about this miracle is the fact that Jesus declared He was going to raise Lazarus from the dead *before* He actually did it. We see this in John 11:4, 11, and 23.

In a similar way, God spoke to Heather Z when she was 12 years old and assured her beforehand that He was going to protect her and take care of her because He had specific things for her to do. That took place about 20 years before a deadly attack came against her life. Here is Heather's continuing story:

> One evening, my husband, Joseph, and I were ministering, and I was really not feeling good. With growing severe pains in my stomach, I told him I needed to go home. Thankfully, the meeting was ending, so I gathered our children and my things and headed home.
>
> By the time I got in the door, the pain was excruciating, and I was doubled over. The pain was so bad that when Joseph came home, I said, "Something's wrong. This is just too painful. I've got to get help."
>
> After making sure our children were taken care of, we quickly left for the hospital. We got checked into the emergency room, and the technicians began checking all my vitals and drawing blood samples to try and determine what was going on.

A short time later, one of the staffers came to me and said, "We don't know what's going on with your stomach or why you're having so much pain, but after getting the results from your blood tests, you cannot leave. You may have to have surgery immediately."

We asked what was happening, but no conclusive answer was given at that time. Another battery of tests was run, and it was now about 4:00 a.m. The severe pain continued. That night in the hospital seemed endless. Finally, the doctor came in.

"I'm so sorry," he said. "I have some very bad news. Joseph, you're going to need to say goodbye to your wife. I don't know how many more days she has to live, but she is going to die."

There we were — stunned, shocked, speechless.

The doctor continued. "Heather, both of your kidneys are failing, and the toxins in your body are so great that we just don't know how long you will have to live. And so, I'm going to give you some time alone."

The doctor then left, and a still silence set in.

With tears now streaming down Joseph's face, he stepped outside of my room for a few moments. At that point in our life, we had a strong understanding that our first response to any bad news is the most important. We had learned that what we say out of our mouth and how we respond in such moments is crucial, which is why Joseph went out of the room without saying a word.

Don't miss this powerfully important principle: **When you receive bad news about anything, your first response to that information is the most important. Life and death are in the power of your tongue, so the first words out of your mouth are vital and can literally save your life.**

Dealing With the 'Death Sentence' of Kidney Failure and Life on Dialysis

How does one handle hearing the news, "You have double kidney failure"? Ignoring the diagnosis doesn't make it go away. So how are we to respond and keep on living after receiving such a devastating report? Heather Z continued:

When Joseph first came back into the room, he didn't say anything. We had been doing ministry for quite some time, and we had learned the importance of controlling our mouth.

He came close to me and said, "I renounce every negative word that was just spoken over you — every word of death, we rebuke it and bind it, and we do not receive that bad report, in Jesus' name."

Joseph then laid his hands on me and said, "You will live, in Jesus' name. You will live in your body and not die, in Jesus' name."

At that point, the doctor sent me home, because there was nothing they could really do. I then began to regularly be tested to monitor the toxin levels in my blood.

Some time passed, and I started feeling very sick again. It was during a season when we were conducting a series of revivals, and hundreds of people were coming to the meetings and getting saved and delivered. I knew in my heart that the enemy didn't want us to continue ministering like we were. Clearly, he was fighting against us.

Just as we were about to get on a plane and leave, I began having such excruciating pain that I had to go back to the hospital. This time they immediately took me into surgery and placed a port in me so that I could be on dialysis. From that point on, for about two and a half years, I continued dialysis about three times a week.

If you're not familiar with dialysis, it is basically living your life being periodically hooked to a machine for hours on end just to stay alive. Large needles, so big that you can see through them, are inserted into the body, and used to siphon all the blood and filter it through a dialysis machine that removes all toxins and excess fluid. It then returns the blood back into your body. The blood cycles through the machine 70 to 80 times during each dialysis session. So with three or more sessions a week, each lasting about four to five hours, being on dialysis becomes like a part-time job to stay alive.

If you or a loved one has been on dialysis, you know that it is a seemingly hopeless scenario. But without such machines, people with kidney failure would die because their kidneys are unable to process the fluid in their body and remove the toxins that build up from the things they eat and drink.

I remember some people who would come in, and in one dialysis session, which was just 24 to 36 hours after their previous session, they could easily take off about 30 pounds of fluid that their bodies had retained from what they had eaten the previous day. The machine is life-giving to those with kidney failure. The big problem is that not only does it filter out the bad stuff, but it also filters out all the good things in your blood as well.

So dialysis was my life for two and a half years. Every other day for four or five hours, I sat with needles in my arms and tubes running in and out of my body. It was exhausting. And like other patients, when I was done with a dialysis run, I went home and crashed, sleeping most of the rest of the day. Maybe I would feel better the next day, but by the time I started to improve even a little, an eerie feeling of fear and anxiety would come on me. Think about it: If you start to feel better, you don't want to go to sleep because you know you have to go back to dialysis the next morning. Thus, normal sleeping patterns were replaced with cycles of erratic sleep and insomnia.

'What Do You Want From Me, God?'

Although God doesn't cause crises to come into our lives, He will use them to recalibrate our hearts and draw us closer to Him. If we will surrender ourselves to Him in times of deep despair, we will experience the richest, most intimate connection and communication with Christ, which is what He longs to have with each of us. Heather Z explained:

> During the first year after the diagnosis, I did everything I could to take in a lot of teaching. I was believing God and doing my best to trust Him for my healing. But after about a year and a half of seeing no change, I became very frustrated and irritated. In fact, I came to the point where I didn't want to hear one more message on healing, because I had heard them all and could quote all the scriptures.

I remember one day I got so angry at God, I said, "What is it, God? What do You want me to do? I know all the scriptures on healing and can quote them, and I've listened to a bunch of teaching and know You're the Healer. What else do You want me to do?"

And He came to me and said, "Heather, you know what I want you to do? I want you to get to know Me."

Get to know Me, I thought. *What does that mean?*

Well, that night I had to be in a church service, and those words kept buzzing in my brain. *Get to know Me... Get to know Me... Lord, what does that mean?*

Then as the music played and the worship team led us in song, I listened as the lyrics began to describe how God holds us in His very hands. Gently, the Lord began to speak to me, melting my heart and reminding me of what He said to me when I was a little girl.

"Remember, Heather," He whispered, "When you died and I brought you to Heaven, I told you I had assignments for you to do? I also said that I would come to you when you needed it and remind you of what I said. Heather, I've got you! Don't worry. You're in the very palm of My hand. Everything's going to be okay...."

Then God said again, "Get to know Me."

From that point on, I scrapped everything I ever knew, and I started to read and learn everything I could about Jesus and having a relationship together with Him. With each passing day, I fell more and more in love with Him. So much so that hearing bad reports about my health didn't even faze me. Rather than being bothered, when I received a bad report, I'd laugh about it. It was just no big deal.

Life went on, and I had the opportunity to meet with a friend who prayed for me, and when she finished, she said, "I know something good is going to happen. I just know it!"

The minute I got home from that visit, my phone rang, and it was my doctor.

"Are you sitting down, Heather? he asked.

"No," I answered. "Should I be?" I didn't know what to think. Was it bad news or good news?

"We have it!" he exclaimed. "We have a perfect match for you!"

I need to backtrack and say that I had had five other attempts in which I was supposed to have gotten a kidney transplant, but for various reasons, it never panned out. It seemed as if my personal scenario made it impossible for me to receive a new kidney. A match for me didn't exist because my unique biomarkers didn't qualify me. Nevertheless, at that moment, my doctor informed me a kidney had been found for me.

"We have a perfect match, Heather!" he repeated, "And you're scheduled to come in this week."

I was speechless. Once again, God was doing a miracle in my life. Indeed, He had me in the palm of His hand just as He said, and everything was going to be okay.

Friend, God's promises can be trusted! The Bible says, "For all of God's promises have been fulfilled in Christ with a resounding 'Yes!' And through Christ, our 'Amen' (which means 'Yes') ascends to God for his glory" (2 Corinthians 1:20 *NLT*). When the Lord promises you something, He will faithfully bring it to pass.

Death Came Knocking… But Jesus Answered Every Time!

It's been many years since Heather walked through each of those life-threatening challenges.

- At age 12, she broke her neck and experienced death.
- At age 23, she faced the death of her first-born baby while in her womb.
- And at age 32, she was confronted with double kidney failure and told she would not live.

But each time death came knocking at her door, *Jesus answered!* Even in all her doubting and crying, her anger and frustration, her questioning and confusion, the Lord never abandoned her. He came through on His promises — not because of Heather's perfect performance, but because of Jesus' finished work and His immeasurable love and faithfulness.

Whatever form of death or deadly situation you are facing right now, God will see you through it! If you're frustrated, confused, or angry, tell Him how you feel. The psalmist David said, "…Pour out your heart to him, for God is our refuge" (Psalm 62:8 *NLT*). Although your feelings may be a shock to you, they are not a shock to God. He is aware of your struggles, so tell Him how you feel.

Realize that every chance the devil gets, he is going to try to lie to you, discourage you, and exhaust you with the things he throws your way. Your job is to *disesteem* the devil's plans and ploys. In other words, whatever words of death he whispers in your ear, *disregard it… discount it…* and *pay no attention to it.* Instead, know what God has promised you in His Word and hold tightly to that!

Believe God's Word Above Your Feelings, Your Circumstances, and Satan's Lies

Whether you feel it or not, you've got to take Jesus' Word above your feelings and circumstances. Yes, you're experiencing real circumstances and you're having real feelings. You can't deny that your situation is real or that your emotions are real. But you can choose to take and believe God's Word (His promises) above your feelings, above your circumstances, and above the bad reports of others.

Heather Z said, "The enemy would bombard my mind with thoughts every week, saying 'You're going to die.' And every time those thoughts came, I learned to say out loud, 'That's a lie! I will live and I will not die!' (*See* Psalm 118:17.) I have life and life more abundantly! (*See* John 10:10.) And God's going to see me through this situation just as He's seen me through all the other ones.'"

That's what it means to participate with God and take His Word above the enemy's lies and above your feelings and circumstances. Remember, you've been in difficult situations before, and God brought you through them. He hasn't changed. He is the same yesterday, today, and forever (*see* Hebrews 13:8). He was faithful before, and He will be just as faithful again to bring you through this situation that seems impossible.

Stay in Your Place of Faith

A major key to experiencing victory is staying in the place of faith. Just as the problem is a real place and the miracle (when the problem is resolved) is a real place, *faith is also a real place*. Faith is the place in between the problem and the miracle. It's where genuine trust in Jesus and awareness of His real love for you is forged in the fire of trials.

When you take and believe God's Word above your feelings, above your circumstances, and above the lies of the enemy, you are staying in the place of faith. Right now, we pray for God's power to be released to you — power to agree with His Word above how you feel, above the circumstances you see, and above the lies of the enemy. In Him, you are more than a conqueror, and you will come out of this as a winner, in Jesus' name!

STUDY QUESTIONS

> Be diligent to present yourself approved to God, a worker
> who does not need to be ashamed, rightly dividing the word of truth.
> — 2 Timothy 2:15

1. Have you ever stopped to think, *What does God know about my life? And what does He think about me?* David answers these questions in Psalm 139:1-6 and 13-18. Take some time to carefully read these verses and journal what the Holy Spirit shows you about God's mindfulness of you.
2. Heather shared how during her struggle for life, she cried out to the Lord and asked Him, "What do you want me to do?" God answered, "Get to know Me." Maybe you know *about* the Lord, but do you *know* Him? What do you think knowing Jesus intimately might look like in your life? What might you do differently in your daily routine to slow your pace and really get to know the Person of Jesus?

PRACTICAL APPLICATION

> But be doers of the word,
> and not hearers only, deceiving yourselves.
> —James 1:22

1. Look back over your life and think of a past situation that was overwhelming and seemed impossible to get through. What was going on? What kinds of negative thoughts and reports were you hearing? What opposition did you face? Most importantly, how did God deliver you and bring you through the situation? And what did He teach you?
2. Heather shared the vital importance of how we respond when we first receive bad news. In all honesty, how would you say you typically respond when you initially hear a negative report?
3. If you can use help in this area, begin to pray, "Lord, please help me! Place a guard over my mouth (*see* Psalm 141:3) and help me be silent and surrender the situation to you immediately. I ask You to give me the desire and power to speak words of hope, faith, and life when I face trouble. I can't do this in my own strength. I'm trusting You to help me *believe Your Word* and *speak Your Word*. In Jesus' name. Amen."

LESSON 4

TOPIC

Forgiveness Opens the Door to the Impossible

SCRIPTURES

1. **Philippians 2:14** — Do all things without complaining and disputing.
2. **Matthew 7:1-5** — Judge not, that you be not judged. For with what judgment you judge, you will be judged; and with the measure you use, it will be measured back to you. And why do you look at the speck in your brother's eye, but do not consider the plank in your own eye? Or how can you say to your brother, "Let me remove the speck from your eye"; and look, a plank is in your own eye? Hypocrite! First remove the plank from your own eye, and then you will see clearly to remove the speck from your brother's eye.

SYNOPSIS

Many of the problems we face in our lives are brought about by unforgiveness. When we hold onto past hurts and refuse to forgive others for the pain they have caused, we unknowingly open the door for the devil to bring various forms of death and destruction into our life.

On the other hand, if we are willing to forgive — just as God willingly forgave us of all our wrongdoing through our faith in Jesus (*see* Ephesians 4:32) — we can close the door on the enemy and open the door to all the blessings God has planned for us!

The emphasis of this lesson:
Like Heather, we are often holding on to past hurts, and we don't even realize it. If we will humble ourselves before God and ask Him, He will show us who we're offended with and give us the grace to forgive them and release them into His hands. The moment we begin to forgive, we close the door to the devil and open the door to God to start working in our lives.

We Need an Ever-Expanding Revelation of God's Love and Faithfulness

On the outside, one who didn't know Heather Z might think she had a problem-free life, but that is far from the truth, as our first three lessons have shown. Her life has been marked by many challenges, including breaking her neck and dying at age 12, experiencing the death of her first-born daughter while in the womb, and being diagnosed with double kidney failure at age 32.

Amazingly, God brought Heather through each of these life-threatening situations — drawing her closer to Himself and proving to her that He is faithful to keep His promises. Indeed, the same resurrection power that raised Christ from the dead was — and still is — alive in Heather, and He is alive in you!

Jesus defeated death in all its forms! And as we live in relationship with Him and draw our strength from His Spirit living inside us, we can overcome every overwhelming circumstance and situation that comes our way. The key to experiencing this life of victory is found in having a real, ever-expanding revelation of God's personal love for us and His faithfulness to keep His Word.

Pursuing a Relationship With Jesus Is the Gamechanger

When Heather received the call from her doctor that a "perfect match" kidney had become available, her prayers — and the prayers of many others — were answered. Yet, as the days of dialysis were coming to a close, there were other impurities inside Heather that needed to be removed — impurities she was not aware of. She explained:

> When I cried out to God in frustration and anger and asked Him what He wanted me to do, He responded by saying, "Get to know me." From that time on, I began to seek Him and learn everything I could about Jesus and having a relationship with Him. He opened my eyes to things I had never seen before — things about Himself and about me.
>
> First, He showed me that although I had memorized a ton of scriptures on healing, they had not taken root in my heart. "You are doing it through *mental assent*," He said. "You have a head knowledge of My promises but are not fully persuaded in your heart that My Word is true."
>
> I knew He was right, but I didn't know how to change it.
>
> You see, I had been listening to hours upon hours of Scripture on audio as well as reading God's Word whenever I had the chance. But eventually I came to the place where listening to scriptures and not seeing any changes in my condition was tormenting me. The reason I was frustrated was because I was mentally assenting (agreeing only in my mind) with what God's Word said. I was not fully convinced and persuaded in my heart that His Word is true.
>
> In frustration, I prayed, "Lord, You're going to have to help me. I really want to believe Your promises in my heart, but I cannot do it on my own."
>
> When I humbled myself and asked for God's help, He very kindly began to move the Word from my head down into my heart, giving me a heart-revelation of His truth. This transformation began taking place when I pushed everything aside and started pursuing a relationship with Jesus.

Heart revelation only comes from abiding in relationship with Jesus (*see* John 15:4,5). There's just something amazing that happens when you genuinely fall in love with Him that can't be put into words.

The Lord Is Able To Search Our Heart and Show Us What's Going on Inside

Along with receiving a heart-revelation of God's Word, there was another major work that God did in Heather's life. As she walked through the process of receiving the kidney transplant and detoxing from all the impurities in her body, the Lord made her aware of some toxic emotions in her soul that desperately needed to be dealt with. Heather continued her story:

> After you get a transplant, you need to take a lot of medication so your body doesn't reject the new organ. In the process, you are changing quite a bit, becoming both irritable and erratic. Little by little, you begin to detox and start feeling like yourself again. It's a transition that is taking place physically, mentally, emotionally, and spiritually. Every part of you is involved.
>
> I remember a particular day when I was really starting to feel good again, and I decided to go for a walk and pray. My husband, Joseph, joined me, but not long after we set out, I just felt like I needed some time alone with the Lord. We had continued doing a great deal of ministry even while I was sick, and I just sensed that something wasn't right in me.
>
> As I walked by myself and prayed, I realized I was frustrated. "Lord, I need some help here," I said. "I'm not really sure why I'm so upset."
>
> At that point, He began to show me that as we had been walking through all the challenges of me being sick and the transitions connected with the transplant, we had also experienced some unexpected drama in the communities where we had ministered. Again, the enemy was not happy about the revival that was taking place and changing people's lives.
>
> Nevertheless, some of the fallout from the difficulties and the harsh treatment we received from others left me quite bitter. In

fact, I am embarrassed to say that while I was walking around that day, I was murmuring and complaining about all the wrongdoing that had been done to us.

To my surprise, as I was walking along muttering my complaints, it suddenly seemed as if the Lord turned up the volume of my words so that I could hear myself talking. As my cutting remarks seemed to get louder and louder, I was deeply convicted and couldn't bear to hear myself any longer.

"Lord, please make it stop," I said. "I can't stand to hear it anymore."

And the Lord said to me, "Heather, just as these people have wronged you, you yourself have done the same thing toward them" (*see* Romans 2:1).

In that moment, God showed me my heart, and I was deeply grieved. Immediately, I prayed, "Lord, please forgive me. I have done the very thing that I'm angry with these people about. I am so sorry, Lord. Please forgive me and change me."

Suddenly, as I began to sincerely repent from my heart, all the seething anger towards our circumstances and my frustration with people began to lift. I was delivered in that moment, and the next thing I knew, I was praising and worshiping God!

The first thing I said to Joseph when I came back was, "I am so sorry for complaining and my attitude of frustration. Please forgive me." I realized that being irritated and complaining doesn't help our relationship with our spouse one bit.

From that moment on, things began to improve dramatically — even in our ministry.

We Need To Deal With Our Own Shortcomings and Let the Holy Spirit Bring Correction to Others

In Matthew 7:1 and 2, Jesus said, "Judge not, that you be not judged. For with what judgment you judge, you will be judged; and with the measure you use, it will be measured back to you." The Lord then goes on to explain how each of us tends to deal with the faults and flaws of others. He says:

And why do you look at the speck in your brother's eye, but do not consider the plank in your own eye? Or how can you say to your brother, "Let me remove the speck from your eye"; and look, a plank is in your own eye?

— Matthew 7:3,4

The reason we often avoid dealing with our own problems is, we are too busy focusing on trying to correct the problems of others. Rather than take this posture of pride and become fixated on judging and criticizing others for their shortcomings, we need to ask God to help us focus on ourselves and address our own issues.

The best motivation for extending forgiveness to others is recognizing our own need for forgiveness. That's basically what Jesus was telling the Pharisees when they came to Him with the woman caught in the act of adultery. As they shined the spotlight on her sinful act, Jesus turned the spotlight back on them and said, "…He who is without sin among you, let him throw a stone at her first" (John 8:7).

When we stop and remember all the mercy and forgiveness Jesus has extended to us — when we realize He was beaten mercilessly, and nails were driven through His hands and feet for all *our* sins — it's a reality check that jolts us out of judgment and enables us to extend forgiveness.

Being Willing To Forgive Shuts the Door on the Devil and Opens the Door to God

Clearly, some offenses are deeply wounding and require a great deal of grace to forgive. In such cases (and in every case), all God is looking for is a willingness on your part to forgive. You can pray:

> "Lord, You know [*insert the person's name*] wronged me, and I'm hurting over what they did and struggling to forgive. But I see in Your Word that I need to forgive. Although I don't feel like forgiving right now, as an act of my will and with the words of my mouth, I choose to forgive [*say the person's name*] and release them into Your hands. Please help me forgive them as You have forgiven me. In Jesus' name."

Friend, that is what it means to forgive! It is an act of the will to drop and let go of someone's offense and surrender the offender to Jesus. The moment we begin to walk in forgiveness, we close the door on the devil and open the door to God's presence working in our lives. Heather Z shared:

> From the moment I began to open my mouth and forgive from my heart the people who hurt me, I experienced a significant shift in my body. I began feeling better immediately and continued to become more and more whole.

Friend, God did not create us to carry around unforgiveness, bitterness, and resentment. When we hold on to these spiritual parasites, it opens the door to sickness and disease. Scientific research confirms that issues such as heart disease, arthritis, high blood pressure, and even cancer are often linked to deep resentment and bitterness in people's hearts.

Your body, your mind, and your heart were created to be filled with God's love and peace. Your choice to walk in forgiveness — to forgive and release those who offend and mistreat you — opens you up to His powerful presence working in and through your life.

Denise experienced the power of forgiveness in her life too. After suffering for many years with painful hands and feet and having recurring panic attacks, she tried numerous things to get relief, but to no avail. Then one day after she poured her heart out to God and asked Him to show her what was going on, He revealed that bitterness and unforgiveness were in her heart. The morning after she sincerely forgave the person who wronged her, she woke up completely free of pain!

Take time now to get alone with the Lord and pray. Ask Him to show you if you're holding unforgiveness in your heart toward anyone. Healing and restoration will begin the moment you say, "Father, I want to forgive [*say the person's name*]. I release them into Your hands. You are the Judge. You have forgiven me much, so I choose to forgive them with the strength You give me. In Jesus' name. Amen."

STUDY QUESTIONS

Be diligent to present yourself approved to God, a worker who does not need to be ashamed, rightly dividing the word of truth.
— 2 Timothy 2:15

1. As a believer, it is vital that you feed your soul and spirit God's Word — and that you *know that you know* His Word can be trusted. Take time to

meditate on and commit to memory these benchmark passages declaring the trustworthiness of the Bible:

> The whole Bible was given to us by inspiration from God and is useful to teach us what is true and to make us realize what is wrong in our lives; it straightens us out and helps us do what is right. It is God's way of making us well prepared at every point, fully equipped to do good to everyone. (2 Timothy 3:16,17 *TLB*)

> Above all, you must understand that no prophecy of Scripture came about by the prophet's own interpretation of things. For prophecy never had its origin in the human will, but prophets, though human, spoke from God as they were carried along by the Holy Spirit. (2 Peter 1:20,21 *NIV*)

2. What is one passage of Scripture that you know God has given you a heart-revelation? What has He shown you about this verse (or verses), and how did He make this truth come alive for you?
3. The Bible has much to say about forgiving others. Take a look at these vital words from Jesus and the apostle Paul and jot down what the Holy Spirit speaks to your heart.
- Matthew 6:14,15
- Mark 11:25 and Luke 11:4
- Ephesians 4:32 and Colossians 3:13

PRACTICAL APPLICATION

> But be doers of the word,
> and not hearers only, deceiving yourselves.
> —James 1:22

1. Heather Z shared that although she knew many scriptures on healing, she only had a *head knowledge* and not a heart-revelation of God's promises. How about you? Are there areas in your life where you have just a head knowledge of God's Word but are not fully persuaded in your heart that His Word is true? If so, in what areas is this happening? Ask the Lord to begin to give you a heart-revelation of His truth.
2. Although we cannot see what is in our heart, God can (*see* Jeremiah 17:9,10). That's why David prayed, "Search me, O God, and know my heart; try me, and know my anxieties; and see if there is any wicked way in me, and lead me in the way everlasting" (Psalm 139:23,24). If something is going on in your

life that you don't understand, pray as David did and ask the Lord to show you what's going on in your heart and what you need to do to make things right.

LESSON 5

TOPIC
Don't Just Hold on to the Power — Give It Away!

SCRIPTURES

1. **2 Corinthians 1:4** — Who comforts us in all our tribulation, that we may be able to comfort those who are in any trouble, with the comfort with which we ourselves are comforted by God.

2. **Isaiah 43:18,19** — Do not remember the former things, nor consider the things of old. Behold, I will do a new thing, now it shall spring forth; Shall you not know it? I will even make a road in the wilderness and rivers in the desert.

3. **Philippians 3:12,13** — Not that I have already attained, or am already perfected; but I press on, that I may lay hold of that for which Christ Jesus has also laid hold of me. Brethren, I do not count myself to have apprehended; but one thing I do, forgetting those things which are behind and reaching forward to those things which are ahead.

4. **Philemon 1:6** — That the sharing of your faith may become effective by the acknowledgment of every good thing which is in you in Christ Jesus.

SYNOPSIS

As believers, we are called by God to represent Him in this world. Second Corinthians 5:20 (*NIV*) says, "We are therefore Christ's ambassadors, as though God were making his appeal through us...." As ambassadors, we are called to show and share with others the good things Jesus has done in our lives. Has He encouraged you, comforted you, and given you hope? He wants to use you to bring comfort, encouragement, and hope to others. Our job is to stay intimately connected in relationship with Jesus and actively involved in the lives of others, pressing on to what God has personally called us to do.

The emphasis of this lesson:

God has called us and equipped us to comfort and encourage one another just as He has comforted us. He wants us to let go of the things behind us and press on to the new things ahead. Our faith becomes most effective as we acknowledge every good thing that is in us because of Jesus.

A Quick Overview of Heather Z's Story

At the age of 12… Heather fell at a playground and broke her neck. Her parents rushed her to the hospital where she died on the X-ray table. The Lord then brought her to Heaven where she came face to face with the brilliance of His presence. While He held her in His hands, He told her, "Heather, I have many assignments for you, and I will come to you again and remind you of this encounter throughout your life. Don't worry because everything is going to be okay. I have you in My hands."

Heather returned to her body, experienced a miraculous healing, and made a complete recovery.

At the age of 23… About 11 years later, she and her husband, Joseph, were expecting their first baby. But about six months into the pregnancy, the baby stopped moving. Three days passed, and Heather began experiencing intense abdominal pain, which landed her in the emergency room for various tests and an ultrasound.

After conducting multiple tests, the ER staff sent Heather home and told her that her doctor would notify her of the findings. But as soon as she got home, her husband, Joseph, took immediate action and began to pray over her. He laid his hands on her stomach and spoke words of health, wholeness, and life over her and the baby.

Very early the next morning when Heather woke up, the baby was moving and kicking again. Soon afterward, she received a call from her doctor who said, "I'm so sorry for your loss. The X-rays and the ultrasound show that your baby is dead."

"No," Heather replied. "Our baby is *not* dead; she is alive! She's kicking and moving all over inside me!" Sure enough, that baby was alive — and still is! Her name is Allison, and she is now a 22-year-old young lady who's married and in full-time ministry. She is a living, breathing example of God's resurrection power!

At the age of 32… Another major attack from the enemy took place on Heather. After dealing with severe, ongoing stomach pain, doctors ran blood tests and diagnosed her with double kidney failure. For two and a half years she was hooked up to a dialysis machine every other day, so that her blood could be filtered of impurities and excess fluid could be removed from her body.

It seems that because her body had built up certain antibodies from carrying and giving birth to her children, she didn't qualify for a kidney transplant. Therefore, dialysis was her only means of survival. In fact, Heather was told that she would be on dialysis till renal failure took her life.

But God had other plans!

As Heather sought the Lord and focused on really getting to know Him, she became fully persuaded in her heart of His love for her and His faithfulness to His Word. Just learning scriptures on healing wasn't enough. Her miracle manifested when she connected with Jesus and He became more real to her than the natural world. Out of that place of being fully persuaded in her heart of what the Lord had for her, her body became compatible with receiving a kidney transplant. Today, she's healthy, whole, and being used mightily in ministry to offer hope and comfort to others who are hurting.

You, Too, Are Called To Comfort Others

Like Heather, if you've been through difficulties in life and have overcome them through God's help and empowerment, He wants to use you to bring comfort to others. The Bible makes this clear in the apostle Paul's second letter to the believers at Corinth where he said:

> **Who comforts us in all our tribulation, that we may be able to comfort those who are in any trouble, with the comfort with which we ourselves are comforted by God.**
> — **2 Corinthians 1:4**

The very same comfort we have received from God, He wants us to freely give to others. You might say we have been comforted so that we may comfort others. Friend, there's a future in front of you, and there are people all around you that God has uniquely equipped you to pour into. So open your eyes and tune your spiritual ears to the voice of the Holy Spirit. He will guide you to the people He's called you to comfort and encourage, using your experiences to bring them hope and deliverance.

God Is All About New Things and Doing the Impossible

Now the enemy wants us to dwell on the pain and problems of the past, replaying every dreadful moment and believing that what has been is what will always be. But that is not the case. The God we serve is the God of *new beginnings*! He says in His Word:

> **Do not remember the former things, nor consider the things of old. Behold, I will do a new thing, now it shall spring forth; Shall you not know it? I will even make a road in the wilderness and rivers in the desert.**
> **— Isaiah 43:18,19**

Looking at this passage in *The Message*, it says:

> **Forget about what's happened; don't keep going over old history. Be alert, be present. I'm about to do something brand-new. It's bursting out! Don't you see it?...**

Clearly, God is into doing things that are brand new and fresh, which is why He tells us to pay attention and stay alert to what He is doing right now. Jesus — the long-awaited Messiah — was living right in front of the Jewish leaders, and they were clueless about His identity. Instead of working with Him, most fought against Him and missed the moment of His visitation (*see* Luke 19:43,44).

Don't let that happen to you.

God is the God of the impossible, and He desires to do impossible things in and through your life. In Isaiah 43:19, He said, "...I will even make a road in the wilderness and rivers in the desert." Have you ever seen a paved roadway in the wilderness? Or a flowing river in a desert? These are impossibilities in the natural, but they are not impossible with God! Jesus said, "...With God all things are possible" (Matthew 19:26).

With God's Strength You Can 'Press On' Through Great Difficulties

It may be that you're in a situation right now where you feel stuck or like you've been sentenced and imprisoned in a dark place and there seems to be no way out. The apostle Paul experienced that exact scenario in real time.

Scholars say that when Paul wrote the letter to the church at Phillipi, he was in a prison that also served as a reservoir for the city's sewage. Can you imagine it? The apostle Paul was in a stone holding tank under the city, literally standing in the sewage that drained down from all those who lived above him. That is where he was when he wrote the book we know as Philippians.

It was while Paul was in this wretched place that he said:

> **Not that I have already attained, or am already perfected; but I press on, that I may lay hold of that for which Christ Jesus has also laid hold of me.**
> **— Philippians 3:12**

Instead of quitting or having a defeated attitude, Paul said, "I press on." He chose to recognize and grab hold of the supernatural power of the Holy Spirit living inside him. Although it seemed impossible, he believed he was going to get out of that horrible prison, which is why he said he was pressing on to lay hold of that for which Christ Jesus had laid hold of him (*see* Philippians 3:12).

Just as Paul's life had purpose, so does yours. God saved you and assigned you to carry out certain tasks, and you are to press on to lay hold of those things. If you will do the difficult, the Lord will do the impossible — creating "rivers" of provision and refreshment in desert places and a roadway out of the wilderness.

All you have to do is take the first step the Holy Spirit is prompting you to take. Then take the second step. He will join you in the journey.

Forget What's Behind You and Reach Forward to the Things Ahead

In his very next breath, Paul went on to say:

> **Brethren, I do not count myself to have apprehended; but one thing I do, forgetting those things which are behind and reaching forward to those things which are ahead.**
> **— Philippians 3:13**

Here we see Paul reiterating and living out the principle of Isaiah 43:18. He is "...*forgetting those things which are behind* and reaching forward to those things which are ahead" (Philippians 3:13). He purposely chose not to hold on to, think about, or lean on his past. He didn't meditate on the bad or even get fixated on the good. Instead, he reached forward to grab hold of the new things that were ahead. We must do the same.

Those who live in the past never take hold of the future. The fact is we are either living in the past or we're living in the present and looking forward to the future.

Faith is not passive — faith is active. Faith says, "I am going to forget the past — I'm not going to mentally dwell on the bad or the good. Instead, I'm going to press forward into the new things God has for me to do."

Interestingly, when Paul said, "I press on," in the original language, it means he was *moving forward with all his might and strength*. It's a picture of a runner who's running a race and wants to win so much that his whole body is leaning forward to get the prize.

That's what the apostle Paul was declaring. He was choosing to forget those who betrayed him, abandoned him, lied about him, and persecuted him. He was even choosing to forget about his prestigious upbringing, education, and societal ranking (*see* Philippians 3:4-7). Why? So that he could intimately know Jesus Christ and fulfill the purpose of God for His life.

The Ultimate Goal Is Knowing Jesus Intimately

Keep in mind that God is no respecter of persons (*see* Romans 2:11). The same power that He deposited into and made available to Paul He has also given to you, which means you, too, have the power to press forward in faith — believing God's Word above your thoughts and feelings, the devil's lies, and your difficult circumstances.

The way you gain and maintain this position of faith is by pressing into God's presence daily, spending time in His Word and in His presence. Reading, studying, and meditating on Scripture is how you wash yourself with the "water of the Word" (*see* Ephesians 5:26) and renew your mind with truth (*see* Romans 12:2).

Additionally, as Heather stated, one of the best ways to experience deliverance is by receiving solid teaching on an ongoing basis from seasoned believers. Just as Paul told people to follow him as he followed Christ (*see* 1 Corinthians 11:1), we can follow mature, unstoppable Christian leaders who are forgetting what's behind and pressing forward to know Jesus intimately.

Acknowledge the Good That's in You

God wants to be believed. He is searching the earth looking for people who will take Him at His Word and become more and more persuaded in their hearts that what He has said He will most certainly do. This kind of active faith attracts His attention and opens the windows of Heaven for His Holy Spirit to really begin working in and through our lives.

Beware of the trap of false humility. It often manifests in our lives subconsciously when we downplay what God has done or is doing in our life, which can include verbally putting ourselves down. Although each of us is a "work in progress," God doesn't want us focusing on our failures and weaknesses. Instead, He wants us to "…[call] those things which do not exist as though they did" (Romans 4:17).

It is the will of God that we acknowledge all the good that is in us because of Jesus. This is how we become most effective. Philemon 1:6 says, "That the sharing of your faith *may become effective* by the acknowledgment of every good thing which is in you in Christ Jesus." In other words, *your faith becomes effective by acknowledging every good thing that is in you because of Jesus.* When you recognize and confess what Christ has given you through salvation, it is an expression of humility that gives God glory.

At the end of each day of creation, God looked at what He made and said it was very good (*see* Genesis 1:10,12,18,21,25,31). His example lets us know that whenever we accomplish something positive, it's important and healthy to acknowledge it. For example, if you've lost some weight because you started eating better, acknowledge it and say it's good! If you did well on an assignment in school or on a work project, take time to recognize it as good. If you pushed past feelings of anxiety and fear and spoke to someone, that's quite an achievement — celebrate it!

Every good thing comes from God above (*see* James 1:17). Whether it's big or small, if something good is happening in and through your life, it's worth celebrating and giving God the credit for it. The more we come into agreement with what God says about us in His Word, the more we are going to see and experience those good things in our life.

For example:

- God says, "You are righteous in Christ" (*see* 2 Corinthians 5:21). So you should say, "I AM RIGHTEOUS IN CHRIST."
- God says, "You are accepted in Christ, the Beloved" (*see* Ephesians 1:6). So you should say, "I AM ACCEPTED IN CHRIST."
- God says, "You are greatly loved in Christ" (*see* John 3:16; Romans 5:8). So you should say, "I AM GREATLY LOVED BY GOD."
- God says, "You are My cherished son/daughter" (*see* John 1:12; 1 John 3:1). So you should say, "I AM GOD'S CHERISHED SON/DAUGHTER."

God knows what He has deposited in you, and He longs for you to come into agreement with Him, confessing all the good things that you have and that you are in Christ. This is a process that takes place as you live in relationship with Him. Every day that you walk with God and renew your mind with His Word, you build a track record of confidence in Him. Friend, if God believes in you — and He does — you can believe that you truly can do all things through Christ who strengthens you! (*See* Philippians 4:13.)

STUDY QUESTIONS

**Be diligent to present yourself approved to God, a worker who does not need to be ashamed, rightly dividing the word of truth.
— 2 Timothy 2:15**

1. Are you in a situation right now where you feel stuck or that you've been imprisoned in a dark place? Take a moment to describe what's going on. How does Paul's situation and his words in Philippians 3:12-14 help you see your situation differently?
2. Not only did Paul forget about all the bad things in his past but also all the good, such as his prestigious upbringing, his societal ranking, and his

religious zeal (*see* Philippians 3:4-6). According to Philippians 3:7-11, what was the driving motivation of Paul's life? How does it compare to David's words in Psalm 27:4 and what Jesus said of Mary in Luke 10:38-42?

PRACTICAL APPLICATION

> But be doers of the word,
> and not hearers only, deceiving yourselves.
> —James 1:22

1. Second Corinthians 1:4 tells us that God comforts us in our times of trouble so that we can comfort others in their times of trouble. Take a few moments to reflect on your life and ask yourself these questions:

   - *What are some of the difficult situations that God has brought me through?*

   - *Who are some of the people God has brought into my life to comfort me?*

   - *Who has God placed around me that could really use comfort and encouragement?*

   - *What life-changing insights can I humbly share with these people who are hurting?*

James 1:17 tells us that every good thing comes from God above, so if something good is happening in and through your life — big or small — it's worth celebrating and giving God praise for it. What are some of the "good things" God has placed in your life because of Christ Jesus? Reflect on the list of things God says about you (in the final section of this lesson) and begin confessing all that you have and all that you are in Christ, thanking Him for actively working in your life.

Notes

CLAIM YOUR FREE RESOURCE!

As a way of introducing you further to the teaching ministry of Rick Renner, we would like to send you FREE of charge his teaching, "How To Receive a Miraculous Touch From God" on CD or as an MP3 download.

In His earthly ministry, Jesus commonly healed *all* who were sick of *all* their diseases. In this profound message, learn about the manifold dimensions of Christ's wisdom, goodness, power, and love toward all humanity who came to Him in faith with their needs.

☑ YES, I want to receive Rick Renner's monthly teaching letter!

Simply scan the QR code to claim this resource or go to:
renner.org/claim-your-free-offer

WITH US!

R renner.org

- facebook.com/rickrenner • facebook.com/rennerdenise
- youtube.com/rennerministries • youtube.com/deniserenner
- instagram.com/rickrrenner • instagram.com/rennerministries_
  instagram.com/rennerdenise

www.ingramcontent.com/pod-product-compliance
Lightning Source LLC
Chambersburg PA
CBHW071650040426
42452CB00009B/1823